Plant Monsters

Contents

Sticky tricks	4
Snap traps	8
Pitfall pitchers	12
Suck, snare and stink	16
Glossary	22
Plant monsters	30

Written by Lindsay Galvin

Collins

Listen, insects! You are too focused on avoiding animal predators. You've been ignoring the plants!

Listen and learn, or you could end up like him.

Sticky tricks

Sundew

Are you thirsty?
Look at those drops of glistening water.
Could this sundew plant share some with you?

Stop! That's not water.

The red hairs hold **globs** of sticky gunk that catch small creatures and clasp them tight.

stuck like glue

Butterwort

This butterwort wouldn't hurt a fly ...

6

Wrong!

It sits low to the ground, out of the breeze. But watch out!

It is covered in **fine**, sticky hairs that **snare** tiny insects.

fine hairs

Snap traps
Venus flytrap

That's a lovely red flower. Let's take a closer look …

Wait!

If you brush past a trigger hair,
a Venus flytrap's leaves slam shut.
But it won't squash you flat.
It wants to eat you slowly.

trigger hair

9

Waterwheel plant

This **swamp** plant will catch whatever small water creature happens to drift by.

A waterwheel plant's traps might not be big, but they are fast!

You can freeze or wriggle, but it won't spare you.

worm

11

Pitfall pitchers

Cobra lily

The scent of **nectar** calls insects inside this **pitcher plant**.

You might think you can escape from the windows, but there's no way out!

Hairs that point down send insects slipping into the cobra lily's trap.

13

Monkey cup

A monkey cup is another sweet-scented pitcher plant. Its cup-shaped leaves fill with water and catch whatever falls in.

ants

It's not just small insects that it can snare ...

Has this tree shrew fallen for its trick?

Suck, snare and stink

Bladderwort

A bladder in a plant is a hollow, flexible bag. A bladderwort has bladders all the way up its stalk.

Bladderworts may be attractive above the water ... but they are deadly beneath!

The bladders suck up water and catch whatever small creatures are swimming in it.

Hammer orchid

Is that an insect perching on a stick?

No! This plant looks just like a wasp.

It attracts a passing male who is looking for a mate. But he soon finds out it was all an awful trick!

19

Corpse flower

The corpse flower is one of the tallest flowers in the world ... and the most smelly.

Its wrinkled petals smell like rotting meat. But this plant is no monster.

It just wants to share its pollen with insects — not eat them!

pollen

21

Glossary

globs thick drops of liquid

fine thin

nectar sweet liquid from flowers which insects collect to eat

pitcher plant a plant with liquid-filled leaves that attract small creatures

snare trap

swamp very wet land

23

Where in the world are plant monsters?

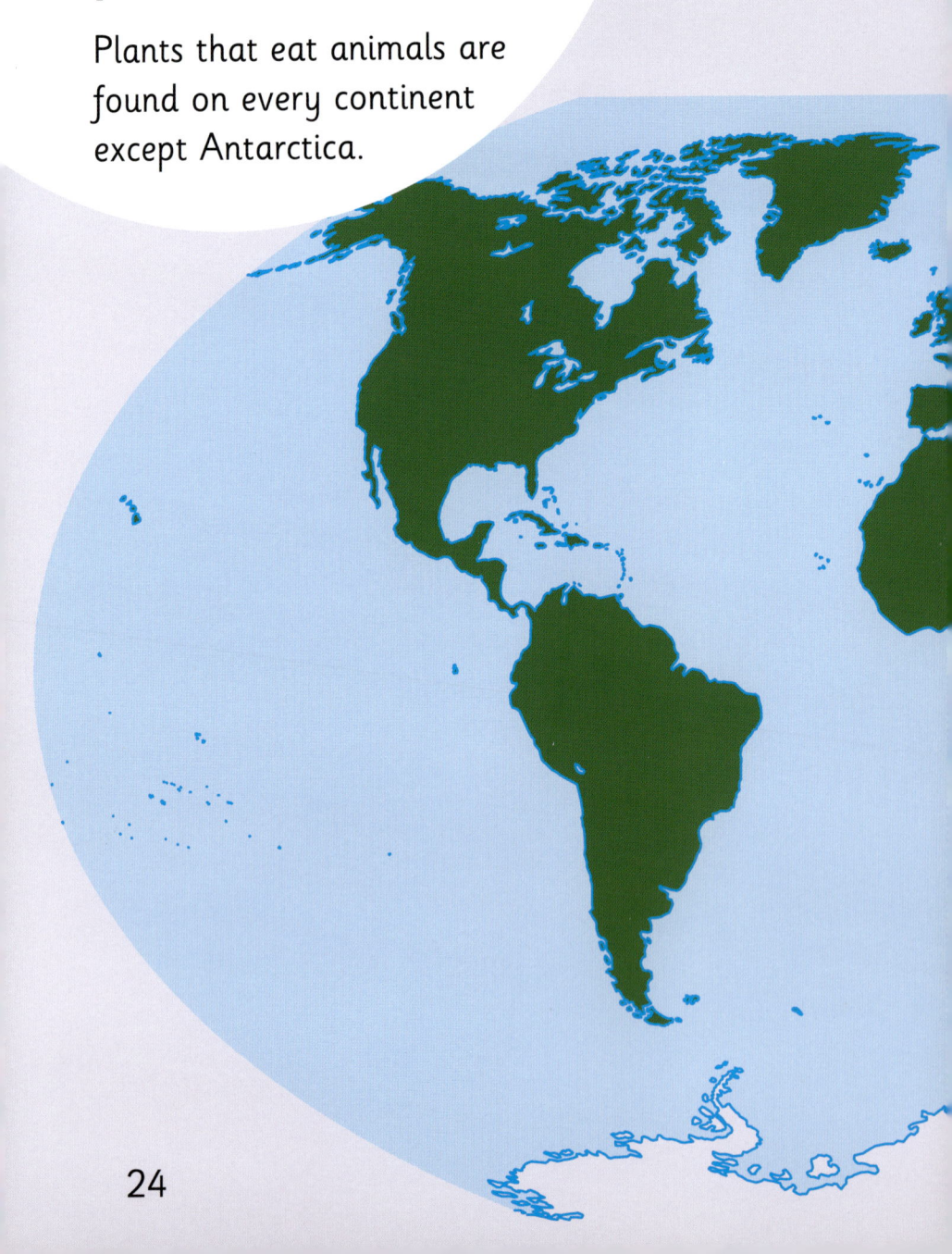

Plants that eat animals are found on every continent except Antarctica.

24

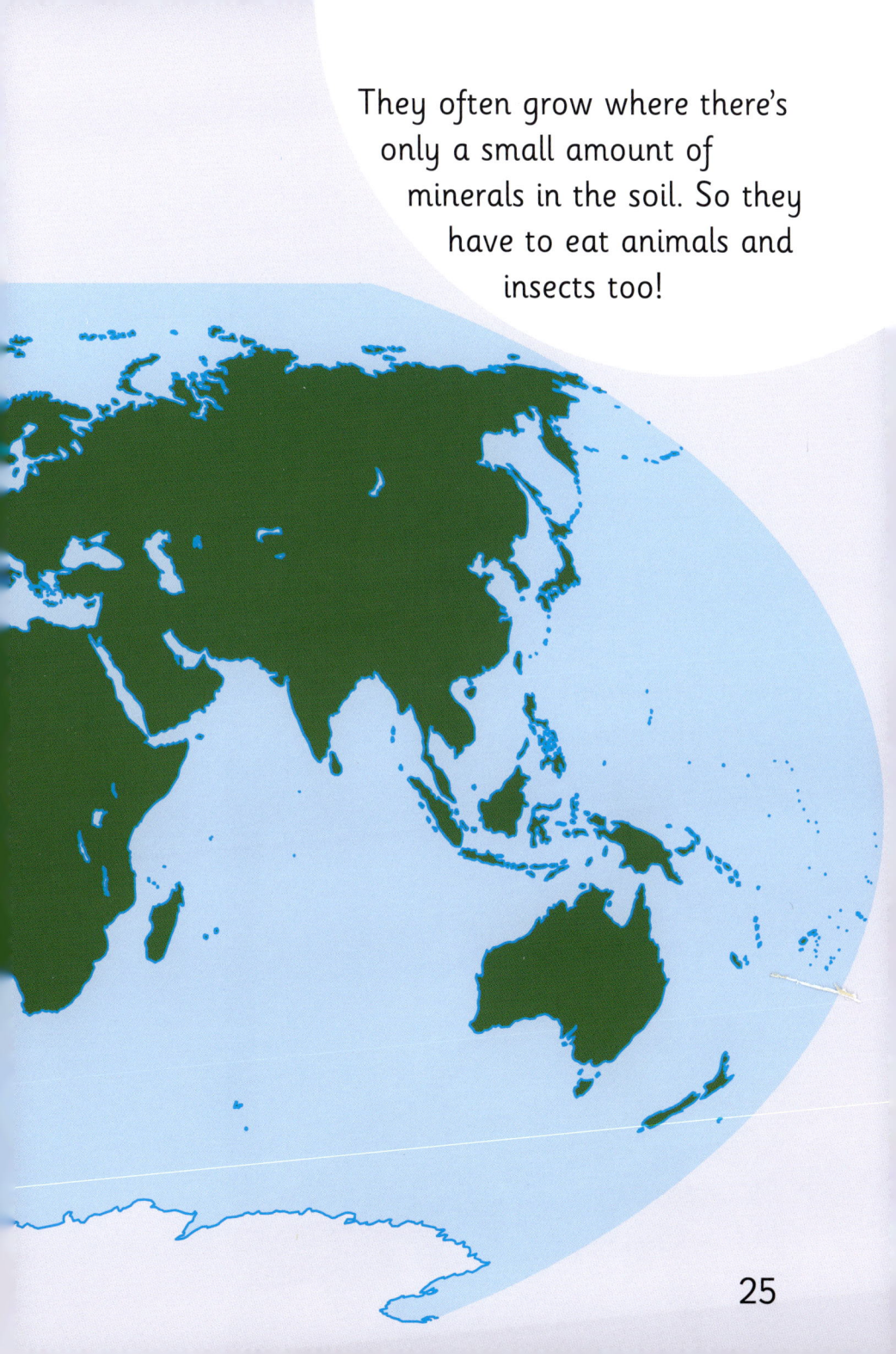

They often grow where there's only a small amount of minerals in the soil. So they have to eat animals and insects too!

Plants to avoid

It isn't only small creatures that need to worry about plant monsters ...

Giant hogweed – causes blistering

Stinging nettles – tiny hairs stick in the skin and cause stinging and itching

Berries — many berries are poisonous to humans. Never eat wild ones.

Thorns — can give nasty scratches — be careful!

Plant monsters

30

31

Review: After reading

Use your assessment from hearing the children read to choose any GPCs, words or tricky words that need additional practice.

Read 1: Decoding
- Ask the children to read the following words. Can they identify the spellings of the /ch/, /or/ and /ur/ sounds?

catch	creature	water	learn
cause	small	predators	

- Challenge the children to read pages 2 and 3 without sounding out. Say: Can you blend in your head when you read these words?
- On pages 10 and 11, discuss the meaning of **drift** and **freeze** in the context of creatures. Ask: What sort of creature might drift? (e.g. *a slow-flying insect, a fish*) Would a creature that freezes be cold? (e.g. *no, just still*) Why might it freeze? (e.g. *out of fear*)

Read 2: Prosody
- Focus on emphasising words to bring out the dramatic meaning.
  - Model reading page 4, bringing out the sundew's temptations by emphasising **thirsty**, **glistening** and **share**.
  - Ask the children to read page 5, emphasising the words that show the dangers of the plant. (e.g. **stop**, **sticky**, **catch**, **clasp**, **tight**)
- Ask the children to take turns to read pages 4 and 5 expressively, emphasising the dramatic words.
- Bonus content: Ask the children to read pages 28 and 29. Say: How dangerous can you make the berries and thorns sound? Encourage them to experiment by emphasising different words. (e.g. *page 28* – **poisonous**, **never**; *page 29* – **nasty**, **careful**)

Read 3: Comprehension
- Ask the children to think about any plants they know that are dangerous. Prompt by asking: What would you never pick and eat? Why?
- Discuss who is meant by **you** on most of the pages. Ask: Who is the narrator talking to? (e.g. *insects, small creatures*) Why do small creatures need to know about plant monsters? (e.g. *some plants feed on small creatures*)
- Turn to pages 30 and 31. Ask the children to imagine they are the wasp narrator, and to put the plants in order of which they think is most scary to least scary. Encourage them to explain their choices.